ALL ROADS LEAD HOME

POEMS BY

NICOLE BORG

Up On Big Rock Poetry Series
SHIPWRECKT BOOKS PUBLISHING COMPANY
Rushford, Minnesota

IN®
DIE

Cover collage by Gwen Elling
Design by Shipwreckt Books

For Lyzander and Lynx

All Roads Lead Home

Part One: Highway 281 & CO-9

Plains and Switchbacks

Out of Kansas

I have become that girl
speaking from behind the curtain—

It is Dorothy I think of and her yappy dog
befriending misfits, taking wrong turns,

trusting in fairy tales to get back home.
I've forgotten home, except in dreams—

the world tears up around me,
the farmhouse flies, and the dog won't stop yipping.

Someone died under a great weight,
someone was bitter and pissed-off and ached inside.

Sometimes, I think I'm the bitter one
or the crushed one or the girl who can't get back.

It's hard to tell with dreams.
Maybe I am none of these—

My heart has turned to tin. I've made an art of forgetting.
I'm always too quick to trust the loudest voice.

Less certain than a road of brick, I will walk a new path,
tracking that wild animal who is me.

I will feed her from my hand
and all that I've never said
                    will come out in a roar.

Strudla

As I was being born,
the women stretched the dough
so thin it could reach from Russia
across the Black Sea, across the Atlantic
to Ellis Island, over miles of fertile prairie
to the Dakota homesteads.

Flour, eggs, salt and water—
my great-grandmother Fredericka
learned from her mother to knead
the dough smooth as flesh,
to pull the dough
thin as the casings for blood sausage,
to bake it with a freshly butchered chicken
to feed the men and children
tired in the fields.

In Grandma Esther's kitchen,
cousin Sheila and I pull the dough
across the big table,
our hands struggling to stretch
but not tear. Grandma helps us
brush the strudla with butter,
roll it into soft cylinders. *Now*,
she says and bows her head,

God is great and God is good.
We're thankful for this food.
By her hand we'll all be fed.
Give us this our daily bread.
Amen.

When We Were Kids

Cousin, you fell down rabbit holes, wandered forests
thick with witches. The moon's darker half
hid the trail that might have led you home.

I caught shooting stars in my hands,
found the end of the rainbow on 11th Avenue,
turned words into tales that shone like gold.

Our stories shouldn't have been so different.
My teen mom and absent dad; your mom the divorcée.
We grew up in the same town at the same time.

The cold of December shrouded your birth.
The moon, when you gave that first cry,
tending toward her darker half.

Our mothers read us different fairy tales—
your mom had four kids, a desk job,
food stamps, depression—

Your jeans were Goodwill, for supper, Captain Crunch.
You wore your parka inside. You waited at the window
under the moon's darkening half.

I never knew how to reach you.
My words lost their magic
outside your middle ear.

I tried to hold you with pinkie promises,
games of Cagney and Lacey, schoolyard songs,
happily-ever-afters not found in books.

We read different fairy tales—I caught stars,
you choked on the moon's darker half.

Barren

At eight, I wanted to be you—
blue-eyed and blonde—
you wore bikinis and Paris runway fashion.
Your long legs were sexy in mini-skirts,
your feet made for heels.
You drove fast cars
with the top down
had all
the accessories.

I carefully dressed you, imagined
your nipple-less breasts
giving cleavage to my t-shirts,
curves to my pre-pubescent body.
Your sex was smooth, unformed.
Even you knew—
the future was barren.

You had everything—
the Corvette and Dream House,
devoted sister, steady boy,
rich-popular friends.

Everything I wanted.
Everything I want.

The Apartments on Teller Street

The divorced mothers leave their daughters
to find their way home—to make an after-school snack
and sometimes Hamburger Helper supper,
to do their homework, or whatever.

On the scarred kitchen table volleyball sign-up,
electric bill past due, black ashtray, Bic lighter,
registration for night school.

Nights alone in the apartment,
daughters lie on hard beds and listen
to the neighbors' music thumping or their lovemaking,
the groaning bed, their unmuffled cries,
or the fights *just like when Dad left*—
her shrieks, his curses, the breaking glass,
his "fuck you" goodbye.

In the living room, her red ribbon watercolor
of a mountain meadow—blue columbine, yellow arnica,
purple larkspur—crooked in its plastic frame.

Behind the gray apartments,
daughters smoke their mothers' Salems.
They check lipstick and sooty eyeliner
they aren't supposed to wear.

They re-read love notes
from the green-eyed jock in Algebra—
he wants me   he wants me   he wants me
They kick rocks with their Payless shoes,
wait for friends to pick them up
                    and take them somewhere.

Mobile Planetarium

The giant blue dome in the gym
is alien to a landscape of fluorescent lights,
white-painted brick, glaring wood floor.
Students line up past the bleachers,
their bodies playful and awkward, never still.

They duck through the flap in the side,
stocking feet scraping the rough, tarp floor.
They arrange themselves in the crowded space,
bumping against each other like atoms.

When the lights go off the darkness is complete,
as if they have been led into the maw of a beast—
something large and hungry, currently sleeping—
they will remember childhood nightmares
and for a moment, be children again.

When the stars appear they are awed,
whether it is *cool* or not to be awed,
and the voice they can't ignore, *Science*,
the bass of James Earl Jones or Martin Sheen,
will command the solar system—
opening it, resetting it to the Beginning—

The Universe being born.
Beneath the brilliant stars,
the girls and boys will exchange a secret brush of hands—
the sky spins dizzyingly, planets appear and disappear,
stars alight then die, suns burn up.

Under Creation's spell, the girls dream
of new galaxies, the boys imagine
bold constellations of light. And the moon's silver twin
blesses their bodies, grown ripe for a first touch,
a first kiss, beneath a star-drunk sky.

In her spring

Françoise in a Round-Backed Chair, Reading.
Oil on canvas by Mary Stevenson Cassatt

Françoise, beside the open window,
reading. The uncut pages lure her
but equally, birdsong
and sun like warm hands
smoothing her hair.
At her back, the lake, blue dream
nestled in grass and yellow-green trees.
Wind brings the scent of water,
moves the curtains,
caresses her skin alive and curious.
She imagines setting the book aside,
a girl's adventure, unlacing her boots,
holding high the frilly skirts of June,
and slipping a foot in.
Her eyes widen with cold,
the way water absorbs flesh,
returns a reflection not quite herself.
Beneath the surface, beneath her toes,
rough sand, stones worn smooth,
plants grown thick tease her ankles.
On the water, undiluted suns dance.
Fish slip past like secrets.
The muddy bottom is a mystery

her feet yearn to know.
Her fingers graze the surface,
trace the waterbugs' frantic dance,
and her gaze, no longer downcast
into words, turns bold, she lifts her face
to the sun, let's it kiss her freely
and wakes to the round-backed chair,
the book open on her lap,
its pages moved by unseen hands.
She inhales the scent of sun-warmed paper,
traces print and pictures—towers and turrets,
clever girl leading the journey, saving her friends.
Distant voices call. She turns away from the lake,
the voices urgent, picks up her story,
gazing down, and begins again.

Stealing the Dream, Pueblo, CO

The girl runs across the mall parking lot,
black hair streaming, pumping arms clutching
Hollister tee, hundred-dollar jeans,
designer leather bag. Behind her the big man
his starched uniform, tinny badge,
sweating brown face. He has stopped shouting.

Across the parking lot stage,
chest pounding, legs cramping, mouth thick with spit,
she eyes the cottonwoods beyond the service road.
She worries the fabric of a t-shirt
like rosary beads.
Mary, Mother full of grace,
Mamí will kill me if I get caught.
Vamonos idiota. Corre. Corre.

The mall cop huffs, but doesn't close the gap.
Stop running, Hija. You can't outrun
this. Minimum wage jobs
and broken promises. After school
and nobody home. You make supper,
help the little ones with homework.
You say your prayers but they're never
answered.

She sprints past cars stopped in the road,
an audience—mothers and kids pointing—
windows down, sunlight in.
Their eyes make no offer. When she passes,
back to their regularly scheduled lives.
She runs, helps herself.

Faith

They worship at the temple
of weeds, beyond the stagnant pool.
Not all believe in *beyond the water*
                    not all jump.
The ones that do twist and writhe,
coil themselves into shapes,
infinity and omega,
and thrusting
break the liquid edge.

> *Their holy book, Ponte Trucha, warns*
> *of land monsters, blurry devils*
> *that choke on water but have mastered it,*
> *lure them with mayflies, mealworms, salmon roe.*
> *Dry promises. Waterless lands.*

Suspended between worlds—
their weightless bodies,
glubbing mouths—gaping eyes see
brightness, color, and
the sense of an *other*,
dark, sleek, familiar.
The Trout of Many Names

> *silver fish, Salvelinus agassizii,*
> *el pez, Mother.*

Ticket Taker

I
This is something you'll be interested in—
the lost year—hospital bed, blank white walls,
footsteps in the hall moving away. Silence.
One spot of blood on a white sheet.
If there were visitors, I didn't recognize them.
If my husband and kids came—I don't remember
why I was there, why I couldn't leave.

II
This is something—kids waiting
in the mall hallway for me to lift the metal gate
to the seven o'clock show. Always, they tried
to sneak into R movies. I called their mothers.
The popcorn kettle's rapid explosions,
the ticket machine spitting paper into my hands
like spent bullet casings. In the lobby,
tinny voices like gods speaking
from far away. War. Buttered popcorn reek
and hot film. Grease-stained white tile,
sticky brown syrup. I counted the dollars
until everything added up.

III

Something—
there aren't security bars
on my apartment windows—
they'd get in anyway. I tell my daughter,
a woman knows when she's been violated.
By who? You live here alone.
My curling iron, missing, the combination
to the safe, changed, the money gone.
My slippers stolen. *How do I know*
what they'd want them for? I say.
I've thought of getting a gun.

IV

This is—the names—*Rock of Ages* and
High Acres Manor. Fuck. Did I used to say fuck?
They take my things—my babydolls, hairbrush,
sweaters—you know, those gals or the old women
and men who shuffle around, mouths agape,
muttering. They look at their hands
as if they've lost everything.

There aren't any mirrors. I don't remember.
What I look like. The black band, shackle,
noose around my ankle won't. Come off.
I've tried. My skin so white. It's winter or spring.
Through the window. The feeders.
Robins open their beaks, sing silence.

The room pictures of strangers are,
their mean smiles, feverish eyes
watch sleep me. I turn my back.
They don't blink. I used to leave to ask.
No one knows. Home.

The bottom dresser drawer,
shoved back, my purse.
Empty checkbook. Paperback romance.
Red lipstick. I put some on before I go always.
Tracing my lips. No mirrors.
Purse in lap. The door. Still waiting.
I'm going out. I've already gone.

Getting into Character

I

At the Loaf 'n Jug in Breck,
Laura and I crowd the counter
and wait, two high school girls
in parkas and lip gloss.
Pack of Marlboros
I say fumbling the words
but the clerk reaches above his head
and hands me a soft pack—
we can't believe our luck.

II

Grandma Esther in a hospital bed dying
lights giving off a urine-colored glow,
machines a-whir, nurses' quiet words
at their station. In her hand, a hair pick
the yellow-green of spring, she plucks her perm to shape,
raises the head of her bed, takes my hand,
Nicky, you're such a good girl.
I stay my tears until the stairwell.

III

My first school play—
in a hokey Queens accent
I audition for Jenny Smith,

struggling actress
whose break comes
playing the Statue of Liberty.
Prop torch raised, book in arm,
foil crown shining—I try not to blink.
I have no lines.

IV
May. Colorado. My back porch.
I light cigarette after cigarette,
inhaling into my mouth but not my lungs,
ashing over the railing into weeds and snow below,
until the pack of Marlboro's is a husk.
I'm getting a feel for this role—
cigarette smoke rising—I gaze
beyond Mt. Royal to stories unfolding,
new scenes, players, speaking parts.

Old Gift

The box has no lock,
just a simple clasp even a child could work.
Your fingers go there, as if to a scar.
You press your ear to the top,
thinking you hear the scraping of wings—
the truth alive, trapped.
It is only humane to set it free.

The box is of old wood polished bright.
You take in your reflection—
your eyes hungry, your color high,
your hands wanting.
It was no different with Eve,
the only fruit in the Garden
forbidden to eat. You raise the lid
and sigh—the golden apple—
round, ready, waiting.

You reach in. Surprised
by its firmness, its heaviness.
That first bite shocks your mouth—
the sweet and the bitter—juices
drip from your chin to your breasts
and your eyes open to the green
of the trees, the dance of light

on the forest floor, your bare feet
on rough ground.

Gold and blue between branches.
All the questions you never asked,
you didn't have the words.
The breeze, cool, raises your flesh,
you cross your arms at your breasts
and hear an unnamed bird—
a glimpse of feathers, small bright body,
perched, head thrown back
singing a tune, no words,
that reminds you of something
you can't live without.

Scientific Method

At the University, she collects
textbooks, credit hours, boyfriends.
Late nights spent studying calculus,
the periodic table, the open mouth of desire.
Her major is Chemistry—
At The Tipsy Sailor she conducts experiments,
what it takes to draw the eyes
of the boys in the low-slung jeans
and backward baseball caps,
their soft hands gripping mugs of dollar beer,
the scent of drugstore cologne heavy
on their brand name shirts.

It's her turn first to perform—
blow jobs before intercourse.
She hasn't found
how her pleasure factors in
except in correlation to his ego,
evidence he has pleased her.

She is doing research—
studying those women on VHS,
testing variables of flesh—
the curves of her body
by moonlight, the pitch of her sigh,
whisper of words in the dark,
meaningless, except of timbre.

   She has always been a good student.

Instructions (for being a woman)

Never fall into routine—
he will know you park at the back
of the Safeway lot, you take the stairs
not the elevator,
you jog on the trail by the river
alone.

When you are out after dark
carry yourself like a man—
back straight, shoulders broad,
face serious.

When you pass by
meet his eyes briefly,
acknowledge don't challenge.
If you sense a threat
make your car key your weapon,
grasp between your first and middle fingers,
stand tall, large, think as loudly as you can

> *I am not a victim.*
> *I will gouge your eyes out.*
> *I will fuck you up.*

Scream. Hit.
Run.

Freshman Year

We settled into each other
as the earth settled into herself,
making love any time of day.

In the canopy of his arms, I found shelter—
Alamosa—a copse of cottonwoods
ready to shed its leaves, rasping of wind
through the Valley, chilés roasting
in a tumbler outside the Mexican grocery,
heads of flowers turned brown with frost.

October was that bareness,
that getting down to the bones—
smooth plane of his skin
(Mt. Blanca beyond treeline)
igniting my body. A raking of coals
blazing red to ash white,
things that stay long enough
to know one another.

His lips, a cold night,
insistent heat of our flesh,
his skin tasting of leaves,

his mouth tasting of smoke.
We traveled a thousand miles in days.

I didn't think what we had
would last one season.

Head-On

The force of the crash,
collision of metal
threw me,
broke and contused me.
Everything stopped.

It will take the Jaws of Life
to get me out of this.

Strapped to the car
to the passenger's seat,
trapped by the guardrail
held in place by the night,
my ride home from college
slumped over the wheel,
forehead split wide
pants dark with blood,
she moans when I shake her.

I didn't say goodbye.
I wanted you to suffer, love.

Snow falls heavy, slow, scatters the red lights,
magnifies shadow, hairline fractures in us.
Low clouds pressing the night into my chest,
mountains moving closer—closed.

Exposed. I shiver.
This new-made convertible
in November. A fireman drapes his coat,
crushing weight on my shoulders.
I lift my arm, painfully point.
"The guardrail ends. We almost went into the creek."
"We would have come down after you," he says.

Stopped
everything.

In my daymares,
I'm taking inventory of my wounds,
reliving—crumpled metal, silence, sirens.
And now, us, on the cliff's edge.
I'm not at the wheel—I stomp the brakes,
lay on the horn, brace for impact.

Warning: The Poison Is the Antidote

Keep out of the reach
of small children, pregnant women,
those with weak immune systems,
impaired judgment. Use only
in emergency, after you've tried
everything, twice.

This emotional cancer, chronic
self-doubt, crushing expectation,
the black eye and bruised ribs,
scars of an ugly childhood,
lies they said and you believed.
You need the strong medicine—
(those marks on your arms,
all the battles you've fought and lost)
the venom, the radiation—
that which kills, saves.

Remove gray safety cap, expose the needle.
Visualize yourself the last time
the smile touched your eyes,
you didn't wake up afraid,
you held your own gaze in the mirror.
When you're ready to risk everything,
place the tip on your chest against your heart.

In some studies
Side effects may include

Be still.
Breathe into the pain.

The world dims, grows light, stars crowd your vision.

Avoid alcohol, cigarettes,
sudden movement, the operation of table saws.
Seek medical attention for prolonged
numbness, chest pain, weeping.
Expect feeling to return to your fingertips,
toes, your heart. Look for purple crocuses,
egrets in flight, the first orange of sunrise.

Slipping Under

I'd never heard the water keen like that.

My dream that night, while you were driving to me—
the lake's cold depths and my foot tangling
in plants grown thick and strong on the bottom.
I watched myself twist, watched my dark hair swirl
around dream-me as she tried to propel herself up,
kicking, struggling, then grew still.

The first nine hours of driving are easy
until you hit that lonely stretch of Nebraska,
turtles crossing the highway by the Platte River,
tires flinging one into space. The rumble strip woke you
when your eyes grew heavy in South Dakota,
when the night was thin as a dream
and the chaste moon offered little light.

You came to me at my parents' barely past sunrise,
a late birthday present, you offered yourself to me.
The lilac blooms had expired, the trees were heavy
with new leaves and green was all around.

You leaned on the doorframe and your mouth found mine.
Later, we went to the dam with Jen, launched her parents' boat.
She steered while we sat close under the hot circle of sun,
not speaking over the whine of the engine and the slap of waves.
Off the island and in rough water, I laughed and dove in.

The cold shocked my body. You jumped in
and the cold cramped your muscles.
You thrashed and went under. *Relax*, I said,
swimming over, *lean your head back on me. Try to float.*
You clung to me. The dream was heavy in my mind
and we both went under. My legs fought and propelled us up.
My body struggled under the weight of water,
the weight of your solid bones and flesh,
everything so dense, while sunlight glinted off the blue,
blinding me, and I knew it was possible to slip under
and never go home.

I have heard

there is a Chinese proverb
If you save a man, you are forever
responsible for his life.
I have also heard there is no such proverb,
a romantic lie authored by Hollywood,
the plotline for a B-movie that sometimes
shows on cable after midnight.

The Cloak Fallen Off the World

The magician's girl strode
in blue silk and spangles,
her wide smile a painted taunt,
her blue eyes an accusation.

It was she who pointed me out.
I squinted at the gold-coin spotlight,
black stage, too much heat and light,
sharp smell of sawdust and sweat.

She offered me her arm, helped me climb the steps
to the wooden box—so much like a coffin
up close. My head and feet stuck out.
I stared at the sea of upturned faces, bodiless in the dark.

Dramatic music played. I waited for the saw.
The magician made a show of letting the dull blade
catch the light. His silk bow tie was askew
when he spoke *For my final trick*.

When the magician laid hands on me,
I held back a scream—his hands, cursed.
I had wanted to know his secrets.
I had wanted to know everything.

The motion of his sawing shook me.
His face was wet with sweat. The coldness of metal divided me
and my vision split. The audience cheered.
I haven't been myself.

In storefront windows, on trains, in crowded streets—
silk scarves, stream of dizzying frantic color,
doves' spastic wings, black oil eyes.
His moving hands, white and cold.

Snakeskin Boots

      —the python
      wound through the woods
fat and greasy and slow.
With her father's knife,
     she killed and skinned it,
     cooked it over a campfire
and let its juices run
down her lips.

     —her father
was muscular and arrogant. He said
   Do something with your life.
    You're not my daughter. You make me sick.
     When she told him to fuck off
and he got up in her face,
she took him down with a leg sweep
    from female self-defense class
      taught by the campus police.

     —rent-a-cop Martinez
wrote her a speeding ticket
but said nothing of her father,
bound and gagged
    in the trunk. As he returned
    her license, his erection

                    pressed against
                    his uniform pants
            and when it broke free,
            she used it for limbo,
and got so low she scuffed
her snakeskin boots
on loose gravel.

Sea View

from the painting Good Neighbors by Laurence L. Schultz

If you painted me into your picture
of the house that reminds me of the sea—
green stucco, warm like gulf waters,
purple umbrella roof, front porch orange as coral,
alien as sponge and phosphorescent fish darting.
If I climbed the tangerine steps—
three to the porch—you would paint me there
in tropical hues.

A sea anemone—my indigo hair, a fan,
my undulating yellow arms,
my rippling red legs.
I empty all air from my lungs
and drift to the sandy bottom,
to the cool deep, to the heavy quiet,
to the painted dark. I settle into myself,
small and dense, still as anything in the sea.

Part Two: Highways 115 & 285

Desert and High Desert

Palm Reading

I can tell you things,
she said, taking my hand,
tracing the lines, following
the shape of my palm,
narrow lengths of my fingers.
This isn't like science.
I'll tell you what I see—
   You have the protection
of air, you will always
be protected—that's in your palm
and fingers. You are open,
a good listener, you can keep a secret.
This line parallels your lifeline—
someone watches over you.
Marriage and children are here,
this cluster. You have a star shape,
a bullet mark near the center
of your palm—that's important.
   Your right hand
is the life you're living,
your left is a carnival mirror—
the life you could live,
if you were brave enough.

The Borders

She is not in Mexico
though she has passed
through the iron gates
and declared her status, *visitor*,
to the Mexicano who eyes her passport
and her face.
This is La Frontera.

This is not Mexico—
the sweating streets,
potholed, honking cars,
cumbias, vendors like locusts,
children yelling *Miss*, waving chicle,
offering to take her photo
for a dollar.

This is not Mexico
her broken Spanish
works here. The taxis
drop the güeros from California
at the discotecas to drink cheap Coronas
and Hennessy, to dance
until her feet can't.

In Not-Mexico,
the night, unsteady.
Taxis wait while she eats
a footlong with jalapeños
and beans, queso and onions
from a hotdog stand after the clubs close.
She drinks Coke from the bottle,
is almost sober at the mirage, La Linea,
clogged with cars, noise, lights—
drunk Americans crossing back.

At La Frontera,
she does not leave the streets for turistas,
she does not go to the part of the city
that is almost Mexico,
where old women sweep the sidewalks clean
and children with scuffed knees
play soccer in dirt
and men in worn boots study the empty skies.

Life 101

My first weeks in California, I am satisfied
by a jangle of keys, two bedrooms, on-site laundry,
four blocks from my school. I sleep on an inflatable mattress
under central air thrumming. I've brought with me
one carfull—computer, clothes, books—my life, boxed.

My first paycheck buys groceries,
Tide, a vacuum, six pack of Henneiken.
Red Hot Chili Pepper's *Californication*.
I splurge on sunglasses with big frames and purple lenses,
pretend I'm a movie star displaced in the desert.

I get news of Colorado from my parents
and ex-boyfriend. My uncles call from Oregon,
my college roommate from Texas.
Even my dad in Fargo phones.
Otherwise *My Apartment of Silence*.

Monday nights I watch *The Simpsons*
from my thrift store chair,
while I correct essays. Fridays, take-out,
carne asada tortas from Mexico Lindo,
a bottle of wine from Vons, whatever is on sale.
This *Routine of Weeks*.

In January, I have a SoCal tan, rollerblade
down Holt Avenue past lines of perfect palm trees,
wave to students, practice my Spanish.
When my seventh graders discover I am single,
they offer to introduce me
to "the one white guy" they know.

Weekends,
I wander Costco and speak to no one,
eat Broccoli Au'Gratin Rice-A-Roni for supper,
go to the bar, dance with strangers.
When the bouncer at Coyote Wells
sneers at my Colorado license,
I am furious. Past one a.m., the Mexican checker
at the 7-11 calls me *mija*, and I want to
throw my arms around her neck,
invite her to IHOP
for conversation and un café.

This Body

She's been waiting
to get back to this body,
to get out of the skull box,

top heavy, goal-driven.
She needs to get back to this
body, to re-enter it like cool water,

easing into its depths,
moved by its changing current,
baptized by sensations of flesh.

She needs to get back to this
body—she used to know how to wear,
loving the fit of her skin,

perfect tee-shirt-and-jeans ease.
Loving her smallish breasts,
round of her butt, curve of her hips.

Loving the length of her legs,
the set of her chin,
her experienced hands.

Loving how this body
lost caution and thought and time
remembering ways to touch—

hands fisting hair, tracing pecs,
mouth on throat, teeth nipping jaw,
fingers gripping shoulders, arms—

and be touched by him—
lips and fingertips and heated breath.
Reborn into this body.

Proposal

Summer vacation has our pockets full of teaching money—
this is our first stop—a fishing town
built on steep hills and water's smooth edge,
feels more like New England than California surf.

We decide against camping, get a room at The Anchor
two blocks from the ocean. We stroll the boardwalk
past paint-peeled boats and quiet gift shops.
Salt wind blows my hair in both our faces.

The Rock is a mesmerizing giant, rugged island,
humped and leathery-back of water troll,
beautiful in afternoon sun. I point to a narrow road.
I want to get married on that rock.

He laughs and pulls me to him.
At a restaurant on the water, we order shrimp
and white wine and eat too much. We speak
in undulating tones, our sandals toe-to-toe under the table.

We go for a walk after dark, buy microbrews
from a frowning corner store. Outside, light ascends from
humid ocean air, I taste rain on the breeze.
Fog moves in like silence, fringes of dream.

At the motel, the T.V. doesn't work. We lie in bed
and imagine our wedding—the fairy tale cathedral in San Diego.
Soft rain and thrash of waves lull him to sleep.
In darkness, I kiss his forehead and listen to his even breath.

July Wedding

          On the Vegas Strip,
the beautiful people are everywhere—
they dress in gold lamé,
they sport their khaki shorts,
they wear their cut-off jeans,
they strut in hoochi skirts,
they glide in Vera Wang gowns—
they're all ready to hit the town.

The sun is hot and always shines
on the beautiful people strolling by
the Little White Chapel
and the Graceland Chapel,
the hotel chapels
and the drive thru chapels.
Elvis gives away a Chinese bride
and they cheer.

The beautiful people fill the streets
and surround the cabs,
descend on the man waving pamphlets
of naked women, spread-eagle for sale.
In the heat they glisten
like the neon at night,
like the Luxor's roving spotlight,

fountain spray dancing
to a thousand choreographed lights.

With their beer bellies and pot bellies,
taut tummies and belly rings,
babies in slings and cameras out
and ready loose change
they welcome us to the City of Sin—
Marriage Capital of the World—
they just want to win.
They aren't ready to leave
            double down
until the money runs out
and their luck too.

Las Vegas Ghosts

Who are you Donald Borger? My hotel room door, ajar.
Red lipstick warning on the bathroom mirror.
Alarm clock backward-racing. Every light on.

Down. I take the elevator, track you
to the casino floor, maze of metal clinking and clanging,
internal machinery wrong gone.

In Caesars' funhouse of mirrors, I catch a glimpse.
The bray of an alarm startles me. Red lights flash
the scene of an accident, a crime.

Metal spews from the mouths of quarter machines,
everyone turns to cheer. I slink away,
a Tanqueray and tonic in my hand. I can't remember.

Ordering. I step through paper scraps of horse race bets,
weave past a cocktail waitress smiling, bustier and fish nets,
blackjack dealer nods as if he knows me.

Security can't find you, Donald, cameras recording every step.
The casino guard suspects me, eyes me out of the corner
of her sly wrong eye, stalks me through showgirls

red feathers, shimmering flesh—a too young Sinatra
croons from the lounge—I palm a bared breast, feel warm lips,
brief slip of tongue, break out in sweat.

From backstage, I stumble into light. Dizzy.
No windows or clocks, here, night never stops. In my defense.
I toast the crooner, tip the waitress. Raise a glass, toast myself.

Street Artist, Balboa Park

He balances the stones
one on the next,
small atop large,
then small, then large
repeating the pattern
until the tower is toddler-sized
and perfectly straight.

The silence of stones speaks.
Their balance and heft
poetry
for his hands
that read desire in rock
unmindful of gravity's restraints.

He works from his knees,
hero pose, *Virasana,*
torso balanced above strong thighs
as he measures the weight of a stone,
finding its center,
nudging it into place
atop a rock round as a nickel
and almost as flat.

They are bound

to Newton's laws
but also to those of God.
They rise into the blue day
like prayer.

He wonders
at the perfection of rock,
unyielding yet malleable
beneath his steady hands
that recognize hope
in what forgives
the least.

To Whom It May (not) Concern:

I am writing this letter to resign
the current position, which in some way
does not suit. I am resigned—of that much
I am sure. It was nothing you did,
in particular, or perhaps
it is that you did nothing, or little at best.
I am confident, however,
the current situation cannot be remedied.

I appreciate the opportunity, of which
I did not take advantage.
I hardly stayed long enough
to make any difference,
about which I am not entirely
indifferent. In fact, as I read
these words, I can't help but feel
there is something we are both missing
in the white between
these lines (I hesitate
to point this out). I have
no doubt, however, that you
will find a well-qualified candidate,
and I, another job

that fails to satisfy. I do expect
to come highly recommended.

Best wishes to you, and good health,
winning lotto numbers,
guilt-free masturbation and world peace.

Sincerely,
N.

New Age

Welcome to the D-Wave Two! Ten million dollars will buy you the thought-ride of your life. This trip is feline-friendly. Make sure your virtual seat backs and trays are in the upright and locked position before take off. In this superposition, your cat is both dead and alive simultaneously. Can I get a meow?

The Captain assures us the revolution against logic has begun. We're currently at 49 degrees N. and 122 degrees W. The air temperature is just below absolute zero and the questions keep rolling in—cure for cancer? Maybe. Self-driving cars? Working on it. Precision forecasting? Got you covered. Key to crack all codes? Kitty, look out!

In this reality, Tom will be your tour guide. So, sit back, close your eyes and enjoy the probability that this ride won't end in fiery destruction on a mass scale. Please bow down to the niobium-chip-brained common gods no longer operating under binary constraints. And thank you for traveling Quantum Lines, where we take you to infinity and back and maybe up to hell after that. Can I get a meow?

Altitude Sick

I met Jesus
at the foot of Crestone Peak
practicing his craft.
The Sangre de Cristo Healing Arts Hut
the sign said.
Jesus smiled and shook his head.
Things aren't any different.
We're all still searching.

He recognized me
though I dyed my hair
and changed my name.
Before me he knelt, gray eyes shut,
fingertips light on my wrists
taking my six pulses.
He scrawled notes, consulted text.

When he touched my feet,
tracing circles and lines
with his thumbs, I cried out.
You have to let go of the anger.
Or do something about it.

He held a tender spot,
the valley of my foot,
and my eyes teared. *I don't know how.*
I couldn't tell him I'd already packed—
my poetry in liquor boxes,
clothes in lawn bags,
left my couch on the curb, *Free,*
disconnected my phone.

To my third eye point
he touched oil
that smelled of lavender,
citrus and scorched sand
and held,
until I was rushing into myself
breathing the thin air, tasting pine.
In sharp relief—the Peak—
my bare feet climbing for the summit.

Curbside Pick Up

Twice a month
we build a shrine on the front lawn
of the little white house we rent—
first, the wine bottles
merlot, chardonnay, shiraz, malbec
at the four compass points,
then brown beer bottles clustered
to earth, wind, fire and air.
We scatter circles of silver,
crushed Coors Light cans,
mounding them in ways
pleasing to the gods.

Bacchus—
let us be merry. Let us find joy
in our libations. Let us bury our sorrows,
the remnants of which lean drunkenly
on the lawn, heads bowed in thirsty prayer.

Spring Flood

Dead fish litter the streets
gutted, heads torn off,

dry scales glint silver.
She walks around the landmines,

their bodies. The streets
have regurgitated themselves,

brown earth and rubble of asphalt.
Stop signs covered in burlap,

crosswalks rain-erased.
There are no safe places,

no avenues through this spring.

The Eve of My 30th Birthday, 10:58 pm

A storm moves in. Lightning and wind.
I'm on the phone with my dad.
I haven't seen him in three years.

We're all getting older, he says.
At sixty, the days go slowly,
but the months and years go fast.

During Vietnam, he joined the National Guard
but didn't get drafted.
He was afraid of going to war,
knew he'd come home in a box.

The wind picks up.
Rain falls like solid bits
of sky pelting the house.

Maybe, he says,
that would have been better.
Coming home in a box.
Coming home a dead hero.

I don't know what to say,
have never known what to say to him.
I sit on the basement steps listening to the thunder
and wait for his *goodbye*.

Miscarriage: A Poem in Two Acts

Scene—
    spring, a Midwestern town
Time—
    the current year

Curtain rises to a woman, alone,
except for darkness

Act I

Early morning sunlight
paints the bathroom orange.
Open window invites robin's song,
scent of lilac, flowering crab.
At a distance, pileated woodpecker
pecks metal, its beak, a living jackhammer.
Count down
t-minus three minutes.
The blue **+** of the pregnancy test
roars—they've been trying—
her hand, almost steady,
she tells herself she's happy.

She crosses
stage left to stage right,
speaks canned lines
to a cast unaware
work-busy husband,
distracted friends,
family too far away.
No one sees—hand to belly—
she never warms.

She carries each scene,
paints emotion with stage make-up—
blush too pink on pale skin,
black mascara, eye shadow a bruise.
She smiles until the smiling hurts her.
Through her town of cardboard
and painted backdrops,
hand to belly—silence
the only real thing in this act.

Act II

Darkness turns to blood,
crimson and warm
soaks her underwear,
cramps come in waves
crashing like music,
like ocean, like birth.

She holds herself
under buzzing bathroom lights,
bleeds through the night,
welcomes the pain,
lump of flesh.
The unborn child speaks
in God's voice
It is done.

Set pieces topple, gel lights crack,
sky breaks open—clumsy hands reach
to comfort her
    to suffocate
She casts off their sadness,
is done with the performance,
leaves before the curtains close.

Outside the air is cool with rain—
she closes her eyes,
speaks her final lines to the sky

    Today, I am baptized in loss. In silence.
    Pain of the maple's first unfurling leaves,
    tulips opening, petals red as lifeblood,
    tender grass, spring's first labored breath,
    these mark my winter's end—
    and in this new day—hope.

Small Griefs

I took it with me—
a little coin of flesh, strange and pink,
not a child yet. Not a child.
I took it with me
in the smallest container I could find,
cradling it in the waiting room,
so the midwife could tell me
what I already knew.

I should have brought it home—
I should have found a maple tree
with somber purple leaves,
I should have knelt
in sun-warmed grass
and dug a hole
just large enough.

Normal

He will be drinking again—
hiding beer cans in dresser drawers
beneath his t-shirts and jeans,
in the garage, shoved in dust-covered boxes,
tossed behind the chest freezer,
under the cotoneaster in the backyard
and the lilac bush that never flowers.
He will go to the bar
and drink alone.

He will forget the car crash,
neck brace and bottles of Percocet,
the rainy weekend in county jail,
Thursday night AA meetings I drove him to,
and afterwards, in bed,
when he spoke to me of addiction.

I will watch him and worry,
swallow accusations, uneasy questions.
I will forget to eat,
nurse headaches like weeds
whose roots hold fast,

dream of him faceless and broken.
I will believe his lies
when things
are normal
again.

Talking to the Dead

The scuttling in the attic
does not sound animal—
when I climb up there's old insulation,
inches of dust and this heaviness
          I can't shake.

Someone has been trying
for weeks to send me a message—
pyramids of coins stacked neatly
in corners, lamps turned on
I know I've shut off, my car keys
missing, toast crumbs on the counter
make the profile of a face.

I mailed one letter to the dead—
Send this to ten people
you love the most, and please,
          don't forget me.

Off-Course

The longest summer
spreads out like an ocean
around the deserted island
your life has become.

You pace the shore, eat
underripe coconut and a cloying
fruit that disrupts your bowels.
You shade your eyes and scan
the sea.
                        Let's be clear—
you are not waiting for rescue.
The paper comes once a week
in a glass bottle that washes ashore—
no news or bad news?

This summer sleep is impossible—
suffocating heat, crash of shadows breaking the shore,
nightmares of twisting metal—
your injured shoulder, burned arm, fractured vertebrae.

Before dawn, you doze, wake
to the taste of beer and stale cigarettes,
a rubber life raft mysteriously
at your feet.   You puncture it,

your sharpened stick digging in,
twisting. Over a fire of twigs
and palm fronds you burn it,
        study the black rising,
the screaming gulls,
sun glaring from the sky, from the sea—

Next morning the boat is back—

You face the water, taste salt on the breeze
and seaweed rotting, consider the current.
You nudge the raft to wet sand and sigh.
You'll fashion an oar, make for the mainland—
There's no choice. You hope for calm seas and
the leniency of the gods.

Therapy

A choir of female conversations
in the large space, peals of laughter
that echo off glass store fronts,
a flash of images—skinny jeans hugging,
designer bag swinging, earrings framing
a well-made face—small packs of women
skimming the glass like a dream.
High heels echo past the sunglass hut,
stall of handwoven hats from Peru,
skin treatment salon camped
in the middle of the mall hallway.
Salesmen reach with slippery smiles.

You don't have to make an appointment
or worry if you see someone you know.
And you don't have to talk
about why you've left three jobs
in three years, why you pace the kitchen
at two in the morning,
why the blank page stays blank.

You don't have to *need* anything.
In the department stores, the lure of perfume,
vanilla and jasmine, softness of Italian leather
shoes, twinkle of gemstones and gold
under well-positioned lights.

A faceless mannequin models
a party dress that makes you sigh.
The scent of French roast lures you
to the coffee shop in the chain bookstore.
You drink. Finger books on display,
shiny covers, bikini-clad vixens,
convertibles, Prada—the promise of love, adventure,
more. Beach titles and thin plots,
you choose one and crack the binding.

The weekend he spent in jail

I popped popcorn and watched the latest
Johnny Depp release (and was disappointed).

There was a lightning storm that night
and the dog cowered behind the couch.

I couldn't talk her out. No one called all weekend.
I ate cereal for dinner and breakfast.

I tried not to think about where he was,
what he was doing, was he going to make a habit of jail.

When I lay down in our too-big-for-one-person bed,
I pictured us—how he'd take my hand

on our walks by the river, or play guitar
singing "Far Behind"

or summer evenings how we'd watch the sun
sink behind bluffs. In bed, I imagined

the comforting weight of his arm around me,
the sigh of his breath on my neck,

his warm presence in the dark—
I thought of him sober and decided to stay.

The Art of Crying

It's best to start quietly, Sister,
if you can, soft as spring's rain.
Don't hide your face.

If it's been a long time
go somewhere—a funeral
or elementary school or hospital.

That first burn behind your eyes,
eyelids blinking, then the spill,
warm on your skin, vision blurring.

Cry like a child hiccupping
and sniffling noisily—
tears as a performance piece.

Or cry like your father
turning his head and
pressing at his eyes.

Cry like your cousin does
chin quivering, noise
in her throat like moth wings.

Cry until your chest breaks open—
everything you've locked there
freeing itself at once.

Let grief make you nauseous,
double you over in pain—
cry, until you're empty.

A blank canvas.
An unstruck chord.
Your hands tremble above the keys.

All Roads Lead Home

When she's driven all night
and the only thing keeping her eyes open
is the radio that cuts in and out,
the stars have receded to backstory,
her coffee is cold in the travel mug,
she can't feel the wheel beneath her hands.

She's awoken to her own unhappiness—
her chaotic job, her husband's drinking,
her family distant, her notebook's empty pages.

Now she's leaving the mountains for the plains,
driving toward her childhood—romanticized—
her grandparents' old house, pink Huffy adventures,
days spent with cousins—one endless summer.

She yawns, blinks hard, imagines deer in the ditch,
their glowing eyes, danger at every crossroad. Weary,
she drives toward her future—what could it hold?

Just when she's sure night will never end,
she notes a graying of the dark
that gives simple shape to the fields
and farmhouses and empty road.

Now the radio picks up the crop report—
prices of wheat, soybeans, corn—
and the sun's first glow warms the horizon.

She knows robins are singing-in the morning,
women are making coffee, men are putting out the dog,
people are stepping into their work clothes
and into their routines. Soon, she will too.

The sun unveils itself setting the horizon to flame,
and it's hard to look away from all that beauty—the flat country
and the green fields, the wide trees and sleeping towns.
The sky that isn't blue yet but will be.

And she knows she's chosen the right road,
she's still the heroine of her story,
driving all night into this magnificent sunrise.

Part Three: Highway 61

River Valley

Expecting
for Lynx

Don't
leave your baggage unattended.
Do report suspicious activity. Would
you care to purchase more leg room?
Carry on bags
must   fit   here.
Please remove all electronics.
Place your shoes in the bin. (Please).
No more than three ounces. Belt off.
Jacket off.   Everything.   Off.
Step
to the side. Ma'am. (Please). There
has been a delay. Something
is arriving. Someone is arriving.
Passenger
_____ to Gate B14. *Those with small children—*
The stewardess doesn't like you. *In case of emergency*
secure your own oxygen
mask first.
This is your Captain. Speaking. There
has been a delay. *Were you expecting?*
The Federal
Aviation Administration cautions
there is no smoking on the plane. The FAA

warns   the pretzels are stale.
This is all you're getting. The passenger
beside you   hasn't showered in three days.
Would you care to purchase more oxygen?
          It is a Federal Offense
to tamper with restroom smoke
detectors. This is not a window seat.
This   is not   a window.
                    What are you looking at?
The seatbelt light is on. And on. *This*
is your Captain speaking. We should
          touch down
some time.
When removing items
from overhead bins, remember
everything   has   shifted.

First Marathon
for Glen

Beneath his worn Mizunos
State Street is straight, smooth,
unforgiving. The impact of each step
moves through the bones of his feet,
ankles, calf muscles, his damaged knees,
tight hamstrings, every cell.
He keeps in back of the pacer,
her yellow stocking cap bobbing
under her raised sign
and tries not to think
    four hours of running

On the sidewalk crowd
women, men, kids
in winter coats, gloves
place-dancing to keep warm
clapping, whistling, waving signs
    You've got this!
    Looking great!
    Keep it up!
Support system of strangers-become-family,
their energy makes him believe.

Away from the starting line
one step at a time
one foot in front of the other
the quiet and the distance, this,
his path alone.
The Oriole's song, flute-like,
almost stops him.
No orange in the trees
but he knows it's there.
He relaxes.
Breathes.
Opens himself to stillness.

                              Hypnotic,
the pace, his feet pounding pavement
endlessly as water smoothes rock,
smoothes what is rough in him.
Fire blooms in his chest, spreading warmth,
he shrugs out of his jacket.
The morning tastes of change—
dew, yellowing grass and damp earth,
dust of broken leaves in the gutters,
maples, elms, oaks ablaze red-orange-gold.
     This is living
not the dark places where lost people
hunker inside themselves
finding ways to keep the night at bay.

On a lonely stretch outside of town,
his left quad cramps, blisters howl
from his feet, lungs burn, his mouth
full of copper, breath comes too quickly.
Grimacing, he squints into
the late morning sun and limps on.
He's lost sight of the pacer.
           He stops in the road
stretches his quads, rubs his calves,
paints New-Skin on his heels, eats a packet of gel,
looks at the
road, field, sky,
gets his bearings.
Breathes. *It's this or chaos.*
He's already drank its dark medicine.

Four months now, he's been training his body
to forget the ways he's abused it,
training his mind to believe in marigolds
like tiny October suns, sweatshirt-clad kids
chasing balls, shouting, back porch barbecues,
laughter. He breathes, claps his hands together
      I've got this
he's never run this far, claps his hands together
      In my dreams I have
One foot in front of the other.
One day at a time. Slow on the downhill.
Steady on the uphill.
Courage for the next curve.
Never worry about the finish.

Día de los Muertos

Each November
we share the food
of our sacred dead—
tortillas and chicken mole,
haloopsa with sauerkraut,
vanilla ice cream and rhubarb—
telling the stories of those
for whom we say a prayer,
bring a photo, light a candle.

Our house is too small—
the kitchen filled with friends.
They serve themselves
from crockpots and casseroles,
tupperware containers,
then crowd around the table.
Placements overlap, elbows bump,
mismatched silverware clanks
percussion to the music
of conversation and children's laughter.

There is room here
at our table—
I hold this moment,
taste it   tart as rhubarb sauce
sweet-bitter
as chocolate and chilés
and give thanks.

Orion

for Lyzander

I have loved you
since Astronomy in fourth grade,
since I could pick you out
of a messy lineup of stars.

For so long, I thought the Big Dipper
was an old fashioned ladle for water.
I never mistook you
for anything but a man—
three bright stars, your great belt,
your broad shoulders,
your bronze club raised.

I told myself a story of you—
As long as you are in my sky,
I said, *I am home.*

You followed me through seasons
and latitude lines,
shifting quietly in the dark,
your eyes unwavering
as any anxious father's would be.
I bore your son,
all light and myth.

Messenger

Her dad's cell number
is always changing and he never
answers his phone. At the crow-tone,
she leaves words for deaf ears.

When he calls, he asks about
the Christmas gift he didn't get—
pictures and a DVD of his only grandson—
did it get lost? She wants to tell him
to ask his wife, arm of the law
that dictates his life. Instead he fixates
on the job he hates, four hours of dusting
the college library. From their perch,
the books glare down at him.

Through the window
she watches crows in the black walnut trees,
their sharp cries like tiny arrows.
He says he's lost two days
this week, now the crows are calling
them back. *Is it the stroke?* she asks.

He thinks it's boredom, all that dusting,
and he would have called sooner
if he hadn't lost his address book again.

He tells her he didn't do anything
on his birthday except listen to the birds.

The crows shriek their warning
but she can't see them now
high in those bare brown branches.

What she wants to ask is
Where did it all go wrong?
She can hear the message of the crows
urging him to stand up for himself
or take flight into the wide blue future
on very uncertain wings.

Promise

for Lyzander and Lynx

You are on loan to me, Son,
for safekeeping (in the stronghold
of my heart and the rooms of
our home), until which time
you absolve our agreement
and take ownership of yourself.

Let my hands be light
and willing to hold, let my eyes
recognize your significance daily,
let my ears open to your heart
that direction your path may take
which is not my choosing,
let my lips make no promise
except to love and protect
as best I can.

This agreement needs no signature
but as such is recognized by the Law
and the Gods, by Woman and Man.
My only wish that your time here
give you strength and vision,
our love a platform from which

you may leap.

Final Stretch

We make our beds, we turn off
all the lights but one.
The garden goes to rot, we pile leaves
when the winds begin to gust,
when we know we'll let the grass spoil
beneath. We bleach towels,
mop floors and our distorted reflections in them.

Headlights only reach so far—
the bright stars, holes in our chests.
The radio, fed from miles of darkness,
cannot fill this. We fold clothes
and untangle cobwebs clinging
to corners and spin them into thoughts
that spill out as words to cover
the refrigerator's buzz
and moan of the furnace and cars
passing in the night.

We pack the bags
we don't take with us.

35th Anniversary Cruise

The trip of a lifetime—
Alaskan adventure—

By the marble staircase and potted palms,
they smile for the camera,

his black bow tie jaunty,
her silver dress reflecting light.

She married the slot machines,
and he, plumbing; but no more.

This is after the scans, tests
between chemo drips,

before Hospice.
With empty umbrella drinks,

they pose in the dining room—
platters of steak, chicken, ham,

crab legs he can't keep down.
They're on a new ship but it's a doomed voyage—

the passengers take ill,
the crew keeps to their quarters,

the Master goes missing.
The ship sinks slowly in friendly waters

with much coverage,
commentary, costume change.

Finding Your Voice

after Susan Chambers
for Mike and Kristi

You need a husband who doesn't read poetry
but believes there is something to what you do
that keeps you up at night,
a husband who will buy you a writing desk
so beautiful you could cry.

You need a grandfather,
retired too early to his grave
to have read anything you've written,
and a grandmother who has forgotten you,
her family, herself, so you could remember.

You need a journal of unlined pages
soft as new leaves, smell of pepper
and dusty libraries and fall and cut wood.
You need scraps of paper—envelopes, napkins,
even the backs of your hands where ink stains your skin.

You need a window to look onto
a maple tree or fat dreaming clouds
or the side of a brick apartment building,
an alleyway, a busy street.

You need a constellation—Orion,
Son of Fire—to root you to the sky,
whose stars, sturdy as nails, ground you
on those chill October nights
when all you have is words.

You need a colicky baby,
for hours inconsolable
in your arms, to teach you
of *hunger* and *need*.

Dear K.,

You keep your cats.
Having a man is overrated. Even on those
lonely nights, the cats will give better comfort,
a quiet understanding or cry with you in *yaos*
of feline sorrow. The boyfriend who spurned you
all those years ago, they would gladly claw his eyes out.
What can a man offer to equal that?

Maybe you thought you'd have children.
Not with the boy who faked his own death and
went to Juvie. A nice Norwegian boy, from church,
and your kids would look like tiny blonde
versions of him, but with less body hair.

You never thought you'd have forty-two cats.
That you'd build a house for them,
clawing posts and cat hostels, hidden passageways
and secret rooms for their kitty trysts. You imagine
feline love affairs throughout the house—
at least someone is *getting some*, you think.

I say, keep the cats—
you'll be happier by far caring for them,
doting on them, cleaning up after them
than some dog-faced man.

Love,
    N.

The Affair

She keeps the stack of poetry books
hidden on the shelf of her desk
behind copies of *Writers Digest*.
They rustle their pages, flash
pretty words, dangerous black print.
It is all she can do to ignore them,
to not go to them, wanting.

When her husband is asleep,
the house murmurs in its bedroom voice
she admires glossy covers,
thumbs thin hard bindings,
strokes pages, sensual flesh.

She reads with her hair down,
lipstick, lamp light, malbec.
She reads with her whole body, leaning in,
the poetry warm in her throat,
words igniting her lips, arousing her sacral chakra,
awakening her body, every aching cell.

Each line, a quickening rhythm
her breathing ragged,
tension building in her thighs, chest, navel—
needs beyond husband, home, bills, baby
where every want is intuited, every desire met.

She opens—a flower—
red petals, pistil, silky black stamen—
exploding into bloom.

When she is full and satisfied,
the night round and fat,
she stacks them on their hidden shelf.
They hum while she sleeps
calling her back.

Seasons

for Marge

The summer of his first year
Zander fell in love with the harvest—
Farmers Market under the bridge—
each week something new.

Slender stalks of asparagus,
fat beets brown with earth,
green pearls of peas, carrots fruit-sweet,
fuzzy dragon tongue beans
best eaten raw.

With hungry hands,
he read the Braille of berries—
black caps, Chippewa blue, red Jewels.
Rhubarb, he dipped in sugar,
honeygolds eaten to the core,
watermelon wedges
left him sticky and wanting.

He obsessed over our only crop,
cherry tomatoes, two spindly plants
fruit-heavy, outside our bay windows.
Sweet 100's ready to split their skins
he picked, feeling their weight

in his hands, warm seeds
dripping trails down his chin.

In October when fall fell hard,
he spoke earnestly, baby-talked the tomato plants
limp and leaning, gestured and paced,
cried to us to fix them. While he napped,
we dug them up, buried them in the compost heap,
filled in the two holes—tomato graves.

That empty plot of dirt
he visited each day,
circled like a mourning lover,
knelt in dead leaves, dug into the dirt,
searching for something red and sweet
a promise spoken in the language of summer.

Final Performance Observation

I see myself
as open
>   *the sky, a winter morning,*
>   *sunlight throwing diamonds*
I have not been approached
>   *by squirrels digging*
>   *for nuts in the snow*
Perhaps problems
with staff

I directed
>   *the sun sinking early behind the bluffs,*
>   *shadows long,*
>   *darkness, falling quiet*
I took blame

For such a long time
I suffered
>   *the comings and goings of moles,*
>   *secret lives of deer,*
>   *squirrels raiding the feeder,*
>   *raccoons strewing trash*
No adherence to policy
>   *clear-cold nights and*
>   *the moon's silver smirk*

I met opposition—
snowmelt, mud in streets,
winds whirling plastic bags,
rising river, threat of flood

Fact. I prepare. I justify
sunlight falling through branches

Fact. I accept
branches shiny with rain, breeze shaking slick buds

Fact. I am consecrated
to new green dancing in the trees

Your Student's Safety Is Our First Priority

I wear my holster on my right hip,
just as they taught me at teachers
college. In this emergency drill,
I'll be shooting blanks.

I instruct my students
to no longer be still, quiet,
but a moving, angry target,
duck and run for the door,
break a window in the top corner,
clear the glass, jump through.

I set my feet and
as if in a first-person shooter—
Halo, Battlefield, Destiny—
draw my gun smoothly
and in one motion disengage
the safety. With steady hands
I will lay that fucker out.

With a whoop and a hoot,
the students will toss their pint-sized
Stetsons into the air
and with their Tony Llamas boots,
stomp on his still warm dead body

and they'll go to the hitching posts
for their horses and ride off
into a bloody red sunset
that smells of gun oil,
hot metal and justice.

In the aftermath

for the students and their families and the faculty of
Marjory Stoneman Douglas High School
February 14, 2018

of another school shooting,
my words try to escape me
like students fleeing
a blood-stained hall
but my pen fells them
like the white male's gun—
stops them in their Nikes

I'm done pretending
the bodies vanish
when the news cameras
leave
My pen can make them stay
prone and prostrate
open-eyed, still
twenty more (or less)
school children ripped apart
blood, red
as a Valentine's heart

They say an AR-15
leaves a body rent, as if
a grenade hid inside the child
and detonated

Tell me, do the parents
identify the pieces
of their shattered
everythings?

This is not a tragedy,
this is a travesty,
a massacre of Innocents
at a school/night club/concert/
theatre/mall/church/street
Breathe

This hate does not discriminate
it's wide as a spray of bullets,
a bullet-bouquet
Senators, we do not want
your "thoughts"
your "prayers"
You have done enough-nothing
Enough

This war with our own humanity
we are losing
I have the right to not be afraid
does that make me weak?

On my lips the names
of dead children
I whisper like a Psalm,
a salve,
like a death sentence
or a pardon

Meditation of the Tradesmen

They arrive when the sun
is new in the sky. Dusty ball caps
sit low on their heads, their boots
make heavy sounds on the hardwood.
They carry in drills and saws,
tape measures and power tools,
a ten-foot baseboard heater
ease into a choreography
of a single human machine.

These men are blunt surgeons
with rough hands,
assessing eyes that take in
the slanted walls, uneven floors,
nothing in plumb. Their soft grunts
challenge gravity and physics
and the rough science of old houses.

Their low voices are intimate—
Bobby, Bucky and Trav.
There is constant diagnosis and revision
feed that bastard through,
little more to the left, almost, no, no, too far
Jesus, Mary and Joseph, try it again
Their bodies can't help but touch

in tight spaces, their voices rise
together in physical strain.

I kneel in the dust of drywall
to the music of the reciprocating saw,
crackle of the two-way radio,
watch their hands work miracles,
coax new wire through old walls,
bring heat to a turn-of-the-century bedroom,
bow my head to their quiet laughter,
gentle curses, and am converted.

Recycled

When my four-year-old asks
what I'd like to be when I am

recycled, I tell him a tree.
He frowns, sighs.

But I can feel the cool earth,
my toes pushing through darkness,

burrowing into silence.
I taste lime and calcium,

my raised arms, closed eyes,
smooth face bathed in light.

He wants to be a robo-cat
with metal skin and laser eyes

and weapons—guns and bombs—
and nine lives. He doubts he will.

I see him, a purple crocus in spring
sprouting through rocky soil, or a sapling

in my grove, supple and slim, bending
with wind, budding silky green leaves.

The worst, he says, is if he came back
a blood red steak on his little brother's plate.

Poet's Confession

Bless me Mother for I have sinned.
It has been thirty-two days since my last poem.
Mother, I have worshipped the iPhone,
I have bowed my head to Bravo,
abandoned my writing desk
to Twitter, SnapChat, Instagram,
my status-updated Facebook page.

I have forgotten St. Williams,
the parable of *The Red Wheelbarrow*.

Mother, forgive me—
I have forsaken the pen and paper.
I have coveted other poets' words.
I have taken comfort in tired phrases,
reaching metaphor, cliché.
I have eschewed editing.

I have read bad poetry
and bragged of it to my friends.

Guest Appearance

Dad sits at my kitchen table drinking tea
from the hand-thrown mug, a gift
from an artist-friend, and watches me cook.
This, his first visit since I graduated college.
I chop onion, carrots, fennel for soup
on the bamboo cutting board
Glen brought from Costa Rica.
Though I am not used to being
in the same room as my dad,
my shoulders are relaxed,
the knife moves easily through its work.

He talks about the Amtrak ride—
the discomfort of sitting so long,
how the train was running late
from the start, they didn't offer food
and he had brought nothing with.
Dad jokes with Zander who runs in and out
bringing toy trucks to the kitchen, lining them up,
singing, playing pretend.

My dad's life—a long-running sitcom
I never tuned in to. Twice a year,
I'd make my guest appearance
Christmas Day and in July,

family reunion. Now, in my kitchen
in this present where I am an adult
and he is an old man,
we speak carefully to one another.

Dad eats soup, salad, bread,
cleans his dish, asks for seconds.
I study him, his thick dark hair
white and wispy, he's forty pounds lighter
than the man, the laborer for the railroad
who was always strong, lean,
his muscled arms held out for a hug
or to take my overnight bag.
Today, he stoops when he stands, sways,
shuffles when he walks.
When he goes outside for a cigarette
and tries to shovel the walk, I look away.

After supper he takes pills, for high blood pressure,
for diabetes, for other things. He's come here
without all his medication. His wife, on the phone,
refuses to tell me the schedule of his pills.
See if he can figure it out,
she says and laughs.

Three days into the visit, his birthday.
I make cashew chicken. He eats enthusiastically,
reads the card Lyzander made for him, is pleased.
I tell him we'll go to Wisconsin for dessert.
He dresses up in a button-down shirt, his thin arms

poking out from the short sleeves, he wears a studded belt
like the college kids and a furry Inuit parka
that either came from a department store
or was a good find at the Salvation Army.
I put on big earrings, tall boots over slim jeans,
a trendy hat. We examine our reflections in the mirror.

On the drive, Dad talks about watching the
Twins' games at the bar by his trailer,
drinking the free coffee for seniors at Hardees,
sometimes eating dinner at the soup kitchen.
He walks everywhere, he says, lost his license
after the stroke. Then, he's singing along
In the Living Years on the radio,
laughing at something Zander says
and suddenly it is real.
I don't tell him I'm not sure
I've ever spent his birthday with him.

I buy us apple pie à la mode
and coffee from the pie shop
in Stockholm. Down the street
to Lake Pepin, we walk
to watch the train. We hear it
before we see it. Lyzander
puts his hands over his ears,
Dad stays still, I lean in,
feel the heat from the engine,
the powerful turbulence
that tugs at us all.

Putting Down Roots

for Dag and Diedre

I don't recognize any of the flowers—
the prairie grass looks just like the fields
of North Dakota where I was born.
On the bluff today, there is no wind.
Anonymous plants reach onto the walking path
to brush against me, the enigma.

Ten years is nothing to prairie grass—
it's the longest I've stayed.
In this river valley, everyone should carry
a copy of their family tree in their wallet
next to their doe license. I never know—
overlapping roots, twining branches,
a single canopy—cousins everywhere.
Until my sons marry granddaughters
of the headstones in Riverside Cemetery,
we're not of this landscape.

As the boys fly down the slide
at the park by the train tracks
and toss handfuls of pebbles
into the air, I find seeds stuck to my jacket
from my walk through native grass.
I pluck them from fleece,

four nearly transparent kernels,
set them on my palm
and wait
for the wind to pick up
and take them away.

Signs

One road leads to another
or leads away from roads
I might have taken, had I known.
But Grandfather's compass is broken
or north has shifted by degrees.

That map in my chest,
the one that speaks
in Grandmother's voice,
is calling out directions.
My mesmerized feet follow,
kicking up dirt and dreams.

There is no moral to this story,
at least not in the way
my parents let me believe.
I'm always searching for signs—
a crow's feather flashing
blue in the sun, wind parting
the flax in a confiding way,
dreams I forget upon waking
that ease into my thoughts
          and quickly out.

Résumé

To succeed

Education
Began with my parents. Soft hands tracing lines, opening doors,
nudging me through.
A finger pointing—do the right thing. A finger shaking—
tell the truth. A finger wagging—be responsible and safe;
safety over happiness.

Experience
I quit teaching English—
two years in CA, two years in CO.
I taught suspended students three days.
An MA in counseling I will never finish.
I have been: waitress, Yoga teacher,
assistant director, arts president.
I have one son.
I have a rough draft of a novel and a poetry manuscript.
I sleep well at night.

Involvement
I don't go to church. I don't go to the bar. I have a writing desk
piled with papers. I attend my husband's basketball games
and my son's preschool events.
I go to poetry readings and book signings,
coffee shops and libraries. I take long walks and short.

I write while my family sleeps.
I sit in the silence. I wait.

REFERENCES
Available upon request.
Contact my son. He is four.
Contact my high school classmates—
they thought I would make something of myself.
You might, through a spirit-guide,
speak with my younger self.

OBJECTIVE REVISITED
I walk my road with intent, hearing every footfall—
I write one more line, give one more kiss,
watch one more moonrise over the sugar maple.

cknowledgments

Without the encouragement and love of so many, this book would not have been possible—thank you to my husband, Glen, to my parents, Sue and Alan, to my dad, Bruce, and to my sons, Lyzander and Lynx, and to Sheila Rohrich. And thank you to Emilio DeGrazia; Mary Logue; the Rural America Writers' Center of Plainview, Minnesota, and Dean and Sally Harrington; River Junctions Arts Council's Writers Helping Writers, and Peg Bauernfeind; the Southeastern Minnesota Arts Council for selecting me for an Emerging Artist Grant in 2014; Shipwreckt Books and Tom Driscoll for taking the risk; the League of Minnesota Poets, and Sue Stevens for sharing her family's cabin; David Svaldi and Adams State University; Carol Giem; Kristi and Mike Kropp for their excellent cheerleading; in remembrance of Betty Benner who understood the tremendous value of words and being true to yourself; and to the community of Wabasha, Minnesota, for believing me when I said I was a poet.

The following poems or earlier versions of them appeared in these fine publications: Green Blade, Dust & Fire, Poetic Strokes, Lost Lake Folk Opera, The Crossings Poet-Artist Collaboration, The Talking Stick, Nodin Poetry Anthology 2015, Main Channel Voices, Eclectica Magazine, The Wabasha Herald, Rochester Post Bulletin, and Off Channel. Many thanks as well to the editors.

Development of the original manuscript was made possible, in part, by the voters of Minnesota through a grant from the Southeastern Minnesota Arts Council thanks to a legislative appropriation from the arts and cultural heritage fund.

About the Author

NICOLE BORG is an English teacher, writer, and poet. She has been published in *Lost Lake Folk Opera, Eclectica Magazine,* and *Nodin Poetry Anthology 2015.* She was a 2014 recipient of the SEMAC Emerging Artists Grant. For five years, she was the lead editor of *Green Blade Magazine of the Rural America Writers' Center.* Originally from North Dakota but having grown up in Colorado, Nicole has an appreciation for place—the mountains, the plains, and everything in between. She loves Yoga, cooking and eating, night-walks, and spending time with her family. She now lives along the lovely Mississippi River in Minnesota with her husband Glen and sons, Lyzander and Lynx.

Up On Big Rock Poetry Series
SHIPWRECKT BOOKS PUBLISHING COMPANY
Rushford, Minnesota

IN®
DIE